All Scripture references taken from the KJV of the Holy Bible, unless otherwise indicated.

MAMMON

Dr. Marlene Miles

Freshwater Press 2024
Freshwaterpress9@gmail.com

ISBN: 978-1-963164-38-1

Paperback Version

Copyright 2024, Dr. Marlene Miles

All rights reserved. No part of this book may be reproduced, distributed, or transmitted by any means or in any means including photocopying, recording or other electronic or mechanical methods without prior written permission of the publisher except in the case of brief publications or critical reviews.

Table of Contents

- DON'T IDOLIZE IT ... 4
- HOW IDOLATRY BEGAN ... 9
- NOT BEFORE GOD ... 19
- DETHRONE THEM ... 22
- KINGDOM ROBBERS ... 25
- UNRIGHTEOUS MAMMON ... 27
- SANCTIFY IT ... 36
- NO SORROW WITH IT ... 40
- FLESH WORKS ... 42
- BUT THAT'S MINE ... 46
- COMPETITION ... 52
- DIVINE INSTRUCTIONS ... 54
- BECAUSE OF LOVE ... 56
- MAMMON BEHAVIORS ... 58
- MONEY TALKS ... 66
- ONE MASTER, ONLY ... 69
- BEWITCHED ... 71
- NEEDS ... 77
- PRAYER POINTS ... 80
- *Dear Reader:* ... 90
- Other books by this author ... 91

MAMMON

DON'T IDOLIZE IT

No man can serve two masters: for either he will hate the one, and love the other; or else he will hold to the one, and despise the other. Ye cannot serve God and mammon.
(Matthew 6:24)

Mammon is *the spirit* behind money.

When Mammon, anything, any person, any deity is edified to a *god*-like position, that it is idolatry. This is when a thing begins to affect you and your life. When a deity, a thing, or even a person is exalted to an idolatrous position, it doesn't easily want to step down.

People cannot at all, or at least find it difficult to let go of their idols. Didn't Laban run after Jacob, Rachel, and Leah when they left his place because Rachel had taken Laban's teraphims--, his *idols*? (Gensis 31:19)

The average man going on a rampage in a house because he's angry at, or fighting with his wife, may tear up things, throw out things, but he will not hurt or throw out his *idols*. The TV set, if that's his idol, will be fine; it will stay on the wall or on the media stand, or wherever the TV is displayed. Anything of his, that he deems necessary and important, will not be bothered. But his wife's stuff is another whole story. He may justify in his mind that he paid for it so he can do with it as he pleases. Or he may be resentful that she could afford it and purchased something for herself and may angrily toss it out the door of the house--, to the left.

But his stuff, such as his model car collection that he's had since he was 10 years old, that's important to him. A favorite football jersey that he can't even fit in anymore will remain. *Idols are safe, even venerated if you don't have Jesus Christ.*

A woman could have a tantrum and if angry at her spouse, and if she has watched too many worldly movies, may ruin his things, thinking that's how to get her *groove* back, and never touch her own belongings.

Unless there is a crazy riot in the street people do not usually tear up their own stuff—, their <u>own</u> *idols*.

They say that it is emotionally painful for most people to let go of money, even to pay their bills. It is so hard for people to let go of *idols*.

You can idolize anything or anyone by giving them more importance in your life than they should have. If you put them **before God**, having more importance or esteeming them greater than God, that is idolatry.

If you believe that you get things because of your good luck charms, your lucky socks or lucky cap, or any number of New Age or fetish items, those things are idols to you.

Why do people stay in bad relationships? One such time is when one person in the couple has become an idol, and she just *luuuuvs* that man, no matter what he does or does to her. Whether she chose to idolize him, or he demanded it, or vice versa, it is still idolatry.

Mammon is like that, too; it demands to be idolized, and those who touch it--, those who touch that *spirit*, have touched an unclean thing that demands worship. Yes, there are some things in this world that you should never touch, or touch without permission, or touch without protection. You see where I'm going here?

In the natural, there is a reason why that man has a whole lot of women chasing him. Those reasons could vary, but idolatry is involved in some way. It could be so strange that he idolizes himself, and others buy into it and worship at his altar.

> So God abandoned them to do whatever shameful things their hearts desired. As a result, they did vile and degrading things with each other's bodies. They traded the truth about God for a lie. So they worshiped and served the things God created instead of the Creator himself, who is worthy of eternal praise! Amen.
> (Romans 1:24-25)

HOW IDOLATRY BEGAN

If God, who created us is not the Lord of our lives then we are serving at least one idol. Many idols are created by man. The man thinks the idol will serve him, but he ends up serving the idol. This is why the Word says that we should not make graven images either of Jesus, God or other things. The main reason is that man will end up worshipping the *image*.

And when the people saw that Moses delayed to come down out of the mount, the people gathered themselves together unto Aaron, and said unto him, Up, make us gods, which shall go before us; (Exodus 32:1)

In our world today we see idols as things, items, money, and other people. People such as celebrities are paraded for good or bad reasons in front of us all day long, in the name of news. Politicians become idols and people will argue, fight, and kill to protect someone who doesn't even know them or give a care about them.

Yes, they knew God, but they wouldn't worship him as God or even give him thanks. And they began to think up foolish ideas of what God was like. As a result, their minds became dark and confused. Claiming to be wise, they instead became utter fools. And instead of worshiping the glorious, ever-living God, they worshiped idols made to look like mere people and birds and animals and reptiles. (Romans 1:21-23)

There is a *god* of everything. Every material item on Earth has a *god* associated with it. Celestial bodies have at least one *god* associated with them; we learn that from studying mythology.

Whether that idol *god* associated itself with the item, or whether it was assigned by man is immaterial; there is an idol *god* associated with everything.

For example, when the golden calves were created in the Wilderness by Aaron, that was idolatry because of worship of beasts, but also there is a *god* of gold and every substance, so they were worshipping the beasts, the calves, **and** the gold, whether they knew it or not. Whether they intended to do that or not, that's what they ended up doing.

Unless God is in a thing, acknowledged, and gives the go-ahead, the OK, then you are directly worshipping the thing instead of God. Repeating from the previous chapter: **…there are some things in this world that you should never touch, or touch without permission, or touch without protection.**

We fully know God was not in the golden calves' debacles. Further, we can understand that the people took off their gold earrings, which were historically worn for good luck. The *god* of gold was providing good luck, so these people thought.

Some forms of idolatry are,

- Fetishism, or the worship of trees, rivers, hills, stones, etc.
- Nature worship, the worship of the sun, moon, and stars, as the supposed powers of nature.
- Hero worship, the worship of deceased ancestors, or of heroes.
- Idolatry extends to relationships, celebrities, items of value, children, people, and et cetera.
- I've met several **people who idolize their parents, as well as parents who idolize their**

children. This will only ruin those children and the parental relationship.

In Scripture, idolatry is regarded as of heathen origin, and that the Israelites learned it by encountering heathen nations. Still, today, we think our own kids are not bad--, it's those *other* kids. You will swear that your kid learned certain behaviors from the other kids in daycare or at school.

Where did ***those other kids*** learn bad behavior from? It started somewhere. Parents, don't be surprised at what your kids learn from TV and online, or what they may be teaching their friends.

Idolatry can be learned from parents, relatives, and friends, outwardly or subliminally. *It's our family tradition, we always do this, or we always do it this way.* The way that your family has always done it can certainly be idolatry.

Idolatry can be in the blood, and therefore passed down from generations.

Egyptian idolatry was supposedly rooted out from God's people during the forty years' wanderings but when a thing is in the blood and has been there for at least 3 generations, it's really difficult to get it out. Deliverance is needed. The Israelites were slaves in Egypt for 430 years. You do the math and let me know how many generations that is.

When the Israelites finally got out of the Wilderness they come upon the idolatrous Canaanites, another heathen nation. We can really see here that being saved and still being in the world is hard work, because most people are heathens and not serving the same God, Jehovah. This is why we must witness to others and win souls, especially as we are sent by God. People are perishing without knowing the Lord.

Thou shalt have no other gods before me.

Thou shalt not make unto thee any graven image, or any likeness of any thing that is in heaven above, or that is in the earth beneath, or that is in the water under the earth. Thou shalt not bow down thyself to them, nor serve them… (Exodus 20:1-3a)

Not bowing down to idols is the first Commandment for a reason, and God's people got into the most trouble, most often for idolatry. It was the national sin, and death by stoning was the punishment for it back then. The Babylonian exile was because of idolatry and its purpose was to get idolatry out of God's people.

A person steeped in idolatry may do almost anything for the one they are serving. Does the person think of this evil themselves, or are they influenced by the *god* they are serving to do the evils that they do? The Bible records these kinds of idolatry such as, human sacrifice, necromancy, blood, wine, grain, offerings, meat and burnt sacrifices, singing, dancing, praise, worship, cutting the flesh, music, bowing, and et cetera.

Animals, snakes, and other creatures have been, and some are still worshipped. What is carved on the totem pole of different cultures? People, yes--, but mostly animals. Totems can be found in Africa, Australia, and North America.

People like things they can see and touch more than things that they must use their faith for–, such as God. Ever notice how parents can quickly soothe a crying child, for example by putting something in the child's hand? That occupies the child immediately, and they usually stop crying. This is teaching idolatry. It's the theory behind a lot of toys that become instant sensations and best sellers, the child can put it in his hand and take it with him all day, and possibly sleep with it at night. There you go. We train kids to have idols without realizing it.

How many adults have you seen give a crying child MONEY? I've seen it. Here we go! A grown man keeps his hands in his pockets all day long. He is at work to supposedly do work. Instead, he is jiggling the coins in his pockets. I don't know if he needs to do that to self-soothe, if it was learned as a child, if he just needs a fidget spinner toy. Or, is he keeping his hand on his idol?

Idolatry implies the worship of a deity in a visible form; that seems to be what man gravitates to. In the wilderness they wanted to worship something they could see, instead of the God who had brought them out of Egypt with many miracles, that they had seen with their very own eyes.

Since ancient times the sun and moon have been worshipped, and they still are. Idols become popular and get worship because in the world, that's where the party is. Pageants, parades, festivals, alcoholic beverages, drugs, sex, perverse sex, even orgies–, anything goes. Man wants to be wild with reckless abandon, but still get all the good that God offers. This is double-minded and not possible.

NOT BEFORE GOD

In the New Testament the term idolatry designates covetousness.

Greed is idolatry, greed can be for food, drinks, anything, but especially money and financial gain.

Why can't you get things from God, if you are a Christian? Why can't you get the things that pertain to your life and godliness from God, especially if He already said that He would supply all those things, and God does not lie. Or why do you think you can't? If you want something ungodly or out of season, you won't get that from God; so, what are you asking God *for*?

If you are not a candidate to receive from God, you need to find out why, since all of God's answers to the prayers of His people are, **Yes**, and ***Amen***.

God is gracious, He rains on the just and the unjust alike, so as a saved person in the Kingdom of God you should have no lack, no insufficiency, no deficits, nothing missing, nothing broken. You should both rest and live in the *shalom* of GOD.

You come to God the right way. Get saved and enter into the fold by the DOOR --- not by any other way.

Idolaters can't enter into the Kingdom, idols can't enter into the kingdom, so until you drop the idols, forget about it.

Money is the lowest power, yet it is a power and it must be conquered.

When you are giving yourself credit for everything you have you are half the way to idolatry.

When you are giving money credit for what you have, you are ¾ the way there.

When you are worshipping money for all you have, and all you are. When you feel as though you are a made man because you have money, then you are all the way into idolatry.

DETHRONE THEM

You must **dethrone** your idols, and put Jesus Christ on the Throne of your heart, then you can *enter in*, that is, inherit the Kingdom of God.

Dethroning your idols means all of them. This means you've got to search your own heart to see what is in your soul occupying the place where God should be. Every false *god* wants to be God and wants to take his position in a Christian's heart. Every false *god* wants worship–, your worship, the worship that should be going to Jehovah.

What's in your heart? Pride and perfectionism--, perhaps calling itself excellence? Insecurity--, calling itself pride? Jealousy--, calling itself protective of your relationships? Mammon--, following the capitalistic culture you may live in, calling itself security or success? Whatever is in there that shouldn't be there, and you're saved, has convinced you that it is something else completely. It has convinced you that it is something good, that it is helping you, protecting you, making *you* better or making your life better.

Know this: Whatever is in your soul that is not supposed to be there is recognized by the fruit it produces through you. If you are producing ugly fruit instead of the Fruit of the Spirit, this is how you know what's on the throne of your heart and embedded in your soul.

This is where we will need some one-another ministry, because most folks, me included, can't easily see our own *stuff*. The Holy Spirit can bring us under conviction, or we may choose to get offended. The *idol gods* are causing you to get offended, because the Holy Spirit is letting you know that they are in there and they don't want to be found or put out. Offense is demon *gods* becoming defensive.

Whichever is in your soul to the greater proportion determines whether you will fall under conviction, or rise up in pride under offense and feel condemned. As said, what fruit you bear should tell you what Spirit, or *spirits* are in your soul.

KINGDOM ROBBERS

In the presence of God there is fulness of joy and prosperity, so where is yours? Enter into the prosperous life by GOD not by any other way. You've got to come to God correctly.

The devil comes to steal kill and destroy, but not you, *right*? You don't have to **take** from God to get things, *right*?

Will a man rob God?

If you are saved and in the Kingdom, when you rob from God, you are robbing yourself, and other kingdom dwellers. You are saying you are not on one accord with the other saints of God's Kingdom, and you don't want to be, (Acts 5:1-11).

When you love, **you Give.** Giving is not a struggle for a saint of God, unless that saint is *listening* to Mammon.

The Spirit of God gives; God so loved He *gave* His only begotten Son. When you love, you naturally and easily *give*.

Mammon doesn't give, Mammon hoards; and Mammon is incapable of love. You can love it, but it won't love you back.

GOD is LOVE. Mammon is **not** love.

UNRIGHTEOUS MAMMON

Do not store up for yourself unrighteous Mammon. How can you make Mammon *righteous*? How did Abraham do it?

Abraham's money came from the world, because Abraham came back from the plundering of the kings, (Genesis 14 and Genesis 17).

He came back from Egypt rich. *How so?* He got money from Abimelech who had taken his wife. God dealt with Abimelech, and he let Sarah go and gave MONEY and the equivalent of money to Abraham. Abimelech gave Abraham PEOPLE! He gave Abraham male and female slaves, Hagar included, and livestock. That has got to be the hand of God for the guy who kidnapped your wife to give her back and give you money for having taken her in the first place. And that guy was a king, no less!

Then Abimelech brought sheep and cattle and male and female slaves and gave them to Abraham, and he returned Sarah his wife to him.

And Abimelech said, "My land is before you: live wherever you like."

To Sarah he said, "I am giving your brother a thousand shekels of silver. This is to cover the offense against you before all who are with you; you are completely vindicated."
(Genesis 20:14-16)

Abraham gave a tenth of all to Melchizedek, the King of Righteousness, the King of Salem, (Hebrews 7:1-10).

Abraham's faith and obedience was counted to him as righteousness, (Romans 4:3-5).

Do not store up for yourselves treasures on earth, where moths and vermin destroy, and where thieves break in and steal. (Matthew 6:19)

What would righteous Abraham be doing with unrighteous Mammon? Why should any righteous man have in his possession anything unrighteous? That is pollution. The unrighteous things defile a man. Idols are unrighteous, all of them. Christians should have nothing to do with them--, any of them.

There are some things in this world that you should never touch, or touch without permission, or touch without protection. Abraham's <u>act</u> toward Melchizedek implied, *I've got this thing here, and I don't want any problems from it. Can we get God into this because I don't believe in poverty, but I need money to live on this Earth, and this money came from the world. Can we get God into this, please?*

And I say unto you, Make to yourselves friends of the mammon of unrighteousness; that, when ye fail, they may receive you into everlasting habitations. He that is faithful in that which is least is faithful also in much: and he that is unjust in the least is unjust also in much. If therefore ye have not been faithful in the unrighteous mammon, who will commit to your trust the true *riches*? And if ye have not been faithful in that which is another man's, who shall give you that which is your own? (Luke 16:9-11)

That which is another man's is the ten percent, the tithe. The tithe belongs to God. Tithing: giving Jehovah the right to be **IN MY MONEY** to cleanse it, protect it, to protect me, and give me the power to enjoy it and remove all evil from what has touched it, enchanted, incanted over it, and just by nature of what it is intrinsically, who made it, whose name is on it, whose picture is on it—whose it is. After all, money is engraved. Not just because it is money, not just because it is backed by **GOLD**, but because it is also **engraved**. Money engravers receive awards and are celebrated in our culture. They even sign the money, and the price goes up because of who engraved it. In Bible terms, *to engrave* means to cut into, inscribe deeply, carve, imprint with a sense of permanence. None should wonder that there are so many dead presidents en-*graved* on money.

> Thou shalt not make unto thee any graven image, or any likeness *of any thing* that *is* in heaven above, or that *is* in the earth beneath, or that *is* in the water under the earth,
> (Exodus 20:4)

What does *making friends* of it mean? When you make friends with someone you make peace with them. You are in a relationship like a neighbor, you can dwell together. *"Here is my land, live wherever you like,"* is what the king said to Abraham and Sarah. As you see, the king also gave Abraham **land**. Abimelech *made friends* with Abraham after taking his wife, Sarah and then returning her. That passage doesn't say marry it or make covenant with it, it says, *make friends*, of it. You trust friends. Even on ungodly money it says in God we trust, not in money we trust. Friends of money means that money has been dethroned from being a *god*. From a *god* to friendship is a demotion for Mammon, it has been put in its right place, but not by you, and not by physical force but by God, who has spiritual power over all *things*, including Mammon.

> The LORD said unto my Lord, Sit thou at my right hand, until I make thine enemies thy footstool.
>
> The LORD shall send the rod of thy strength out of Zion: rule thou in the midst of thine enemies. (Psalm 110:1-2)

Until money is brought under subjection, every dollar ain't a good dollar. It's the friendly dollars that are good. Mammon can be programmed to attack you on evil altars; money can be your enemy unless you put it in its right position. Hit men and conmen are paid with money, every day to do harm to people. Mammon will drive people to crime, hate, jealousy, revenge, drug use. Anything unrighteous is an idol and I've said over and again that idols talk. Anything unrighteous will say unrighteous things and urge a man to also be unrighteous.

Hagar was a slave of value, but look at the trouble that arrived when Ishmael got here. Even though that was Sarah's idea for Abraham to impregnate Hagar, Sarah and Hagar were not friends. A non-friend is an enemy. It will want to stay away from you, or Lord over you. After Ishmael was born, Hagar thought her importance to Abraham surpassed Sarah's role. When Abimelech gave that slave to Abraham, Hagar was **legal tender**; Hagar was as <u>MONEY</u>. Look at how money, when worshipped, copulated with, brought forth offspring with Abraham, and then wanted to take over the house. It's because what represented MONEY was never put in its rightful place or taken out of its rightful place. Abraham shouldn't have had sex with Hagar, because that is worship, in the natural. In this case, Abraham worshipped legal tender.

A friend will not urge a friend to do wrong or to sin. A friend will not secretly work against a man to destroy him, slowly or suddenly.

God will make Mammon serve you and not try to attack you, or accept evil programming to attack you, or come back later to bite you. You are *friends*, even though you should rule over it. Is it not easier to rule in a civil setting than in a hostile one? God can make that happen. God can make money answer all things for you.

Wasn't Abimelech still king over the land when he made *friends* with Abraham? He still ruled that land, and Abraham, but he had made friends of him. Like Abraham, when you serve a mighty God, even the kings of a land will live in peace with you and make friends with you. It is because of the Mighty God you serve.

Left to its own devices, without God in your money, the *spirit* of money, Mammon will mutiny and try to run your life.

SANCTIFY IT

Money is the world's system, and it belongs to the world, it comes from the world; it is made by the world. Money bears the image and the inscription of whoever engraved it, minted it, printed it--, who made it.

I am created in the image and likeness of God; God made me. And I bear in my body the marks of the Lord Jesus Christ; I belong to GOD. The inscriptions on and in me do not match that of the world. At least, they are not supposed to.

The devil tries all kinds of evil against man, including evil marks, evil garments, evil ideas, evil acts, and evil human agents may be employed to send curses, like Balam was hired to curse Israel, or they will come personally into your life, on evil assignment to steal, kill, and destroy.

Anything of the world's that I want to handle, use, consume or have--- I have to go through my Heavenly Father for permission and get Him to tell me it's OKAY and let God into it for protection, safety, out of respect and love. That is if I am a true emissary of Heaven. If I think I made myself, sent myself and am not responsible to anyone, including God, I will err and I will not acknowledge God in **all** my ways. That's where we all mess up.

Trust in the LORD with all thine heart; and lean not unto thine own understanding.

In all thy ways acknowledge him, and he shall direct thy paths.

Be not wise in thine own eyes: fear the LORD, and depart from evil. (Proverbs 3:5-7)

We should come to God as little children, and ask permission for all that we do, everywhere we go, and how to go there. No, it's not so God can boss us around, it is for our protection. We don't know what evils lurk around the corner, physically, and in the spiritual world.

And said, Verily I say unto you, Except ye be converted, and become as little children, ye shall not enter into the kingdom of heaven. (Matthew 18:3)

Do not touch the unclean thing.

Wherefore Come out from among them, and be ye separate, saith the Lord, And touch not the unclean thing; And I will receive you, And will be a Father unto you, And ye shall be my sons and daughters, saith the Lord Almighty. (2 Corinthians 6:17-18)

Any of us may be guilty of not acknowledging God in all we do. Growing up we listen to our schoolmates and pals who say, *"Let's do this, let's do that, it'll be fun."* And just like the devil, they may also tell you, *"Don't worry, nothing will happen. No one will know."* Because as children, most of us are not saved and Spirit-filled, so we start listening to the voice of people instead of God. This begins the bad habit of not asking God if we can do, or should do certain things or not.

There are some things in this world that you should never touch, or touch without permission, or touch without protection.

NO SORROW WITH IT

God gives riches and adds no sorrow with it.

If you have money and sorrow has followed it, you have unrighteous Mammon, and it has mutinied. It is talking, saying, B*uy this, buy that. Look at what they have. Go there. Impress those people.* I know a man who traveled a lot. No, it was not his own wanderlust. Wherever his brother vacationed, because that man had to prove he was as successful as his brother, he had to soon copy his sibling.

There are some who, when they get money, must spend it. People say that money is burning a hole in their pocket. That is not literally happening, but all idols seek to influence whoever has their hands on it.

FLESH WORKS

If money is sending you to work your flesh or build up your flesh, you need to get your money saved.

If you go shopping but say, *"I'm going shopping and if this credit card goes through, I'm going to get the outfit, the shoes and the handbag."* You have just asked Mammon for permission to buy clothes and accessories.

I'm going to go get a new car and if my application goes through–, same thing, that's Mammon. That is not making friends of Mammon; that is exalting Mammon to a *god*. Getting permission from Mammon? Or playing the cash register lottery, that is witchcraft.

Did you ask **GOD** about any of these purchases?

If what you put on your credit card is not of God, that is why it is so hard to pay it off. If what has been charged on your credit card has been exalted past God, by not getting God's permission, not acknowledging Him in all your ways, even in your shopping *ways*, then you have exalted either money or the things that money can buy to idols. Or, both.

Oh, you may say I just bought basic necessities. But what is the *spirit* behind the purchases? Why did you buy those certain things, brands, or products? Pride? Do you want to impress others?

You are depressed and went shopping to cheer yourself up, retail therapy? Real peace and lasting joy come from GOD, not from money, and not from shopping.

Mammon will tempt you with lust of the eye. Do you want to look good to others? God adorns us for divine connections and to bring Him glory. Anything else, or anything more may make you into a strange altar.

Lust of the flesh, or any flesh work, such as jealousy–, your neighbor has one, so you want one, or a better one. Those attitudes are Mammon-driven.

You only buy all the best cuts of meat. Your steaks, your salmon cost the most; you won't eat anything less. You don't even eat leftovers – ever, because you have a *lifestyle*. That is your prerogative, but make sure your attitude is not offensive to God. If you are not one to go out and pick your food fresh off the vine, you don't know when the food was picked. If you don't eat leftovers, you do not need a refrigerator. But you have a refrigerator, don't you? So don't be a food snob.

Give God the glory for your food.

Your vacations have to be the best so you can post your pics online.

There is no reason why you can't have nice things or the nicest of things, but it is not to impress others. It is to bless God, be a witness in the Earth, help others, and win souls.

REVENGE: *This will show them.* It's why a lot of people don't have money because of what they will do with it. If you charge something on your credit card for revenge, that is so not of God and if you don't repent it will be impossible to pay it back. If you charge something on a credit card that is not even yours, for revenge, that is even worse.

Repent.

BUT THAT'S MINE

Why do people have such violent reactions to other people getting nice things?

Mammon.

Recall, it is hard to let go of one's idols. It is equally as difficult for some people to see other people doing well **financially**, because they see the successful people as having a relationship with their idol *god* — Mammon. MONEY. This is evidenced in the money the other people either have, spend, use, or flaunt.

An office manager held a barbeque at her house and 8 co-workers came to the event. Four of her co-workers nearly lost their minds because the office manager's home and pool are so nice. Two quit the job because they suddenly hate the manager. One redid her entire house; it took a year. Another stayed on the job but became a sour uncooperative employee, always trying to cast aspersion on the Office manager. The rest were pretty normal.

Which ones were serving Mammon became obvious by their jealousy and change of attitude.

People are so tied to their idols, that it's like having a spouse or a boyfriend/girlfriend and you see them with someone else, they go into a jealous rage. A silent, and sometimes prolonged jealous rage.

It's not like those folks have bought the last nice car in the world, or the last pretty house, it's just that their idol, their secret boyfriend is over there cavorting with someone that's not them.

Maybe they didn't even know that they were serving Mammon. Maybe you didn't even know that you were serving Mammon. Maybe you still don't know. I pray you're not.

When people get jealous because others have money, use money, flaunt money, or have nice things, suspect Mammon worship.

The office manager may not have been serving Mammon, but when a jealous onlooker sees money and *stuff,* they downgrade what they see to only what they see. They are giving Mammon credit for what God may have given someone because money is the onlooker's *god*.

That office manager could be a saved, sanctified, set aside saint of God, totally blessed by Jehovah. Now, ideally the onlooker should ask, *"Who is your God?"* And this should turn into a witnessing opportunity because God's people should always have nice things, or the nicest of things.

In the world, many people who have all the trappings of wealth serve Mammon, and they automatically assume that the same demon *god* that they serve should make them as rich as movie stars, mogul businessmen, and some criminals. They break down what they see to their own lowest common denominator: and that is simply money. These have not made friends of money; they have exalted money to a *god*-like status and without realizing it are asking Mammon into their heart to lord over them. Now, in asking for money all the time, some want to lord over people, but they don't realize they are inviting Mammon in to lord over *themselves*.

This cuts both ways. I know of people who have lost their jobs because they drove their really nice car to work. When their boss has a *pharaoh spirit* and wants to keep them stagnant or subservient, that boss will not be happy to even see their employee doing well.

Lots of people do not drive their nice car to work, but they have a knock around car that they use Monday through Friday for their jobs. The reason they don't is not just to keep the mileage low on their luxury car, but also to keep jealous eyes off of it and keep problems at work to a minimum.

God is not cheap, but what is your *attitude* behind what you do, what you buy, what you drive, how you dress? What drives you to do your hair and makeup? If what you buy with money will distract you from God then that means you will or have exalted either the money, the item you acquired--, or both to *idols*.

It is why some people do not have money and things. God knows they will idolize the money or the things that money buys.

If you are charging *idols* on your credit card, or buying the things that your idols are telling you to get, versus acknowledging God first, how do you plan to pay for those things? Idols never plan to be under you, as you expect them to. Idols plan to be **over** you, as soon as you invite them into your life.

COMPETITION

Your sister has one, therefore you want one, or a better one. No, the *spirit of competition* says you want **two**. So, you start to amass money, money, money, by any means. That's Mammon. You may call it jealousy, but when whatever you are so-called jealous about has to do with MONEY and it always has to do with money, you are serving an idol *god*, and it is Mammon.

Your sister, your co-worker, your office manager has one. Now the competition, the war begins. It might be one-sided, the other person doesn't even know you are competing with them, and they are not competing with you, but it is all you can think about. You are scheming, devising, wishing, figuring.

Where in the Bible did God tell **anyone** to go get something because somebody else had one?

What did God say do? God said, ***Behold I do a new thing.*** He did not say go and copy the old thing.

When Mammon finds out that you will do **anything** for money, it's got you!

DIVINE INSTRUCTIONS

Notice that when God told people to build something, He told them **exactly** how to do it, to the cubit. God did not ask them *how much money do you have*?

Where in the Bible did God give another *version* of the vision? Where did God say, "**Oh since you don't have enough money, let's change those blueprints. Let's change those plans.**" NOPE. Because if He did that would mean that God was asking Mammon what can My people build? That would mean that God was submitting to Mammon, and that will never happen.

God made sure they had more than enough money. God gives the vision; God gives the provision. When money is giving you a vision, whether you don't have any, or you don't have enough, or you have too much--, you've seen some obscene mansions, *right*? --, then, money is the lord of your life.

El Shaddai, the God of More Than Enough will make sure you your church, your ministry has more than enough as long as you are obeying God. Preach what God says preach. Teach what God says teach and God will send the people and supply all your needs according to His riches in Glory. He does that because that is God's church; He will not allow it to fail. When God is invited into a thing and allowed to stay there, God will sustain it. That means churches, businesses, and even you.

BECAUSE OF LOVE

There is he that scattereth, and yet increaseth; And there is that which withholdeth more than is meet, but it tendeth to poverty. The liberal soul shall be made fat: And he that watereth shall be watered himself.
(Proverbs 11:24-26)

That's because he that scattereth, he that gives, has Love. When you Love, you give. You give because you have Love and love is the opposite of fear. If you have Love, it is indicative that you have taken on the nature of what Spirit is in you. If God's Spirit is in you, and especially to the point of taking Godly actions, that is an indication that God has either instructed you in what you are doing, or you are at least acknowledging God to find out what you should be doing as far as the purpose, the vision, and the activities of your life are concerned. This is all in contrast to your asking money, asking Mammon what you must do, or what you have permission, or *enough* to do.

- What's going to make me the most money?
- How can I keep this money?
- How can I do what I know I'm supposed to be doing, but also keep the money?
- Where can I hide this money?
- How can I keep other people's money?
- Money, money, money.

MAMMON BEHAVIORS

Mammon makes you spend wildly, or hold on to money. It can make you fearful, miserly, cheap, evil, and cause you to miss opportunities, blessings, divine connections and messing up relationships ---worshipping that money believing that *money is a god.* Idol *gods* are great impersonators. Idols can't take on the nature of God, but they will try to *impersonate* Him to influence you to do what they want, thinking that you're obeying God. There is a difference, but they've made their decision to follow Satan and not God, yet they want what God has, they want authority, power, and worship. They want God's people. We can't fall into their traps.

You feel safe and secure when you have it; you feel insecure when you don't. You feel powerful when you have it, you feel weak when you don't.

You feel important or good enough when you have it, you are bummed out or depressed when you don't have it.

You feel like the king of the world if you have more than other people you know, but when you have less, or feel that you have less, you don't feel good about yourself or your situation.

Notice how idol <u>*gods*</u> have you living your life by *feelings*. I've said before feelings and *feel like it* are always very expensive, and they are very poor choices.

Once exalted, even by mistake or on purpose, knowingly, or unknowingly, an idol will start to rule your life. It then begins to speak into your ear or heart to give you thoughts, ideas, and to influence you to take on its nature. It wants to live and express the horrible things it wants to do through you because you have a living body on this Earth. What it wants you to do is horrible because it is serving Satan, not Jehovah. It is when you LISTEN to money that you make it a *god*. Idol *gods* talk all the time. Yes, it talks all the time, it tells you, all the more, how to feel.

Oh, I hear you. You may be saying you don't listen to money – no, but are you rehearsing the words of someone who listened to money, who worshipped money? Perhaps it was a parent? Did you inherit this way of thinking? Are you serving the idol *gods* of your father's house? Idolatry can be in the blood, inherited and you may pass it on to your children.

We must pray for our foundations, always.

Saints of God: I don't believe in poverty or vows of poverty, and I certainly don't believe that poor people are holy or holier than rich people. If poor people are so holy, why do they commit so many crimes? Rich people commit crimes, too; sometimes, that is how they got rich.

Money is a necessity of life, but like everything else, it has to be put in its place. **There are some things in this world that you should never touch, or touch without <u>permission</u>, or touch without *protection*.**

If you were the devil and everybody needed a certain something to live and function, wouldn't you find a way to demonize it, and weaponize it? In this way you could get your agenda out there. And, you can control people with something that they need every day. After all, it's going into every house and the longer it stays in that house, unrighteous and uncontested, as unrighteous Mammon, the longer it will talk and spit out its agenda.

Is money wicked? Yes, as long as it is unrighteous. What communion do the righteous have with unrighteousness?

The lust of money is the root of all evil. If money was righteous, then strongly desiring it would not create *all evil.*

What are all the evils? You will find money at the root of any and all of them. As they say in the world, *Follow the money.*

Money carries a *spirit* or *spirits*.

Idol *spirits* are chatty. What do you think those idols will be spouting off?

Bible verses?

Of course not, except to twist them. Sometimes there may be a little truth mixed in with lies, but mostly it is lies, unbelief, fear, worry, anxiety, greed, selfishness, and works of the flesh.

Once you get anything from an idol *god*, once it believes it has done anything for you, then you owe it –, you and your generations, because you can never repay it. Yes, what you do, your decisions even with money will affect your children and your grandchildren.

Once you give it any worship, like a stray cat, it will not want to leave. It will not want to leave its position in your life and your generations.

Man is a generator of worship. You cannot stop worshipping, even if you want to. You will worship something; it's innate and inherent.

You can change what you are worshipping to begin to worship another thing, but you will still be worshipping something. Even when you don't know it, worship can be taken out of you. Especially observing traditions and doing what everyone else is doing, such as what the world is doing is pulling worship out of you to whatever the world is worshipping. It doesn't matter if you even know what you are worshipping. Especially if you don't know that you are worshipping, it is being pulled out of you. For example, Halloween comes to mind. The devil adds fun into an activity. Christians think they are taking the fun out and leaving the devil worship.

Nope, can't be done. When you participate in any way, you are worshipping.

WORSHIP is reverence and adoration to GOD, (or a deity) **that should be God in our case.** Something that demands or gets your attention is asking for worship. You've got your mind on something all day, all night, all the time. Is it God? Or is it some person?

If it is money, then that's Mammon demanding and getting worship.

MONEY TALKS

I keep telling you that money talks.

We see in the movies that drug dealers have stacks and stacks of money in their possession. They have it socked away in their houses, piled up in their mansions, or wherever they live. Where do you think that money has been? In the offering basket at church?

Nowadays--, maybe, but in a real offering basket at a *real* church? Most likely, not.

Wherever it is, money, if it has not been submitted to God, it will talk.

What do you think that money is saying to them?

- You need guns.
- People are after you... you have enemies.
- People want to rob you.
- They are cutting into your territory.
- People want your position.
- People want what you have.
- Don't go to sleep, guard your money.
- You need more guards.
- The people around you cannot be trusted.
- Go buy some flashy cars and clothes and show off this money.
- Go to the club, throw some of this money around; let them know who you are.
- Your wife is cheating on you; you can't trust anyone.

- Oh, I forgot – movies, put this money all over the bed and sleep on it… WORSHIP. That is worship.
- Count me again, and again. Make sure it is all there.
- YOU NEED MORE MONEY, MORE, MORE, MORE.
- Look at me. Admire me. Worship me. That's what Mammon the *spirit of money* will be saying to you.

Seriously, what do you think money talks about or says to people? If you listen, you have exalted paper and metal money to a *god*. Once you obey it, that is worship.

ONE MASTER, ONLY

You should be listening to God, not idol *little g gods*—not money, for sure. Because you cannot serve two masters, you will love one and hate the other.

There is he that scattereth. GOD says give; Mammon says NOPE. God says give $100. Mammon says maybe $5 or $10--, *if that*.

Lay not up for yourselves treasures upon earth, where moth and rust doth corrupt, and where thieves break through and steal:

But lay up for yourselves treasures in heaven, where neither moth nor rust doth corrupt, and where thieves do not break through nor steal:

For where your treasure is, there will your heart be also. (Matthew 6:19-21)

Where your heart is, is what you worship.

Coins & paper –, what *spirit* is on money? You don't know because you don't know where it has last been.

The rich young ruler would not go and sell all he had and give to the poor so he could follow Jesus, but the widow gave all she had in the offering (parable of the widow's mite). Kinda bet you that the rich young ruler's stuff was talking to him; Mammon owned him.

The widow who gave the mite, which was the last coin she had. She was free of Mammon.

BEWITCHED

Money can be bewitched. Unrighteous money can be bewitched. Sanctified money cannot be. Where did your money come from? You don't know because it's been all over the place. You'd better clean it. When I think of how many hands touched the apples that I just got from the grocery store--, ewww! I have to wash my produce.

Regarding money, if the first fruits *be* holy, the lump is holy. Money can be bewitched, enchanted. Don't you know folks who started acting differently once they got some money, and not in a good way? That could be an internal thing, or it could be something on or about that money.

Money is put on altars as sacrifices to the positive or the negative; it does what it is told.

After being enchanted, money can be sent into a person's life. Every dollar ain't a good dollar. The object, money, itself can be hexed, vexed, enchanted, and then sent over into your life.

Money can be an initiation.

A 45-year-old, married man with children goes into a business. There, he sees a young lady, about half his age. She is not a cashier there and handles no money. This man is well dressed, but there is something oppressive and intimidating about him, although he uses no coarse words towards anyone there. He leaves the business, after asking her to be his *friend* and leaves a $50 bill on the counter telling her that it is for her.

I will tell you now, it scared her, and she went to the owner of that business to ask what she must do about this money and that man who frightened her, or gave her the creeps.

That girl should not accept that money. She should not touch it. She should not put it in her purse; she should not take it home. Fortunately, it was found out that the man owed that business exactly $50, and the payment was applied to his account. However, the business owner didn't want to put it with the other revenue that company received for the day, and did not want to put it into the company's business accounts.

First there was prayer to break any curse, assignment, or initiation programmed into that money--, either taking it, accepting it, touching it, or comingling it with any other money.

Personally, I believe that man knew where he was going that day, and who he would see; he was very focused and bothered no one else in that business, although he saw many other people there. I believe he was sent, or sent himself by evil divination.

FYI, it's been close to 2 years, and he has never come back.

So, we must plead the Blood of Jesus over this money, deprogram any curses or enchantments over this money that it will not affect that girl, or anyone else in that company, the business itself, or anyone else who may handle that money.

As I am known to do, I do not let anything that I believe is ungodly come to a higher position than under my feet, so it should have been left on the floor for some days. The current owner of that money did sanctify gain to the Lord, but not that actual $50 dollar bill, but its equivalent in the offering to God.

- Lord, sanctify my money, in the Name of Jesus.

Weeks later, some tradesmen came into the business, and the $50 was given to them as a tip for services rendered. You can see how money goes from place to place, and if not prayed over, *stuff* will remain on it.

Mammon is the *god* behind money, and it wants worship. It is used by people who want worship from other people. Mammon is both used on altars, and it has made itself into an altar, as well.

As long as you are dissing God when it comes to what He tells you in His Word about money, you are serving Mammon. If you are dissing God and listening to money, you are worshipping Mammon.

It is a binary choice; you cannot serve two masters. If you are not worshipping God because you are distracted by money, either because of not having any, not having enough, or having too much –, all of that is worship. If your mind is on money all day, that is still worship to Mammon.

Moderation should be in all things, else Mammon can tempt a person with too little, or too much (Proverbs 30:8)

Mammon has certainly got a demonic charge on it. We all know how it influences man every day. I did not see anywhere else in the Bible where an idol *god* was called a *master*--, only Mammon.

NEEDS

Money got the title of master *or god (little g god)* because it is visible, prevalent and the devil has cleverly tied it to NEED.

The devil creates needs and then offers you **wrong** choices to solve those needs – those problems.

Money comes from the world and is created by the world. We are *in* the world and not **of** it, so we have to consecrate our gain to the Lord to give God the authority to be IN our money to help us, and bless us.

God will use MONEY and turn it to riches and wealth; else it is *just* money and will be *only* money. If you haven't told money what to do, it will do what the last person told it to do regarding you, and that last *person* could have been the devil. We know from Scripture that money is the root of all evil; unrighteous Mammon is a problem to every man's life.

> Arise and thresh, O daughter of Zion: for I will make thine horn iron, and I will make thy hoofs brass: and thou shalt beat in pieces many people: and I will consecrate their gain unto the LORD, and their substance unto the Lord of the whole earth. (Micah 4:13)

> For it the firstfruit be holy, the lump is also holy: and if the root be holy, so are the branches. (Romans 11:16)

Clean it up. Consecrate it. Sanctify it.

If you caught a fish for dinner, would you take the scales off and dress the fish? Whatever evil is on that money you just got is as *scales*. You must take them off before use.

The fish is a gain, but you don't keep **all** of it – some of it has to be removed before it is suitable, before it is edible.

Money is the same way.

PRAYER POINTS

Lord Jesus have Mercy on me a sinner, forgive my sins, the sins of my parents and the sins of my ancestors. Lord Jesus, if I am none of Yours give me a repentant heart and a Godly sorrow for my sins, and make me one of Yours, in the Name of Jesus.

Lord, I ask for the Holy Spirit to a greater measure, so there is no room for any other *idol* on the Throne of my heart, in the Name of Jesus.

Covenants that must be settled before God can fight for me, break, and die, in the Name of Jesus. I AM IN CHRIST.

Every evil covenant that allows entrance of any idol *god* in my life, be broken, dismantled, and scattered, in the Name of Jesus.

I am IN CHRIST. I will not serve two masters; I renounce and denounce all *idols* that I have ever served, Lord, forgive me, in the Name of Jesus.

I cannot and will not try to serve both God and Mammon. Lord Jesus, take your rightful place as the Lord of my life and by my Godly actions regarding money, I put Mammon in its place, in the Name of Jesus.

Mammon, you can be a friend to me as the Scriptures say, but nothing higher. You cannot be my *god*, and I will not marry you. I serve the Most High God, Jehovah and Him alone, in Jesus' Name.

I will worship the Lord and serve Him only.

My Heavenly Father provides for me; I do not need to chase idol *gods*, in the Name of Jesus.

Lord if I have inherited idolatry, cleanse my blood, heal my foundation, in the Name of Jesus.

I seek His Kingdom, and His righteousness, all these things will be added to me.

The Lord supplies all my needs according to His riches in Glory, by Christ Jesus.

I am blessed. My spouse is blessed. My children and my *children's* children are blessed.

My business is blessed.

Everything I put my hand to is blessed. I renounce all greed, selfishness, and selfish ambition, all boasting and envy.

My stuff will perish; it will burn--, but my Father Jehovah rules and reigns over all, in the Name of Jesus.

With a heart of thanksgiving, I pass through the gate of approach to the indwelling Holy Spirit.

With a heart of praise, I enter into His court. I tender the sacrifice of Christ; I enter in-- I confess, renounce, and repent of my sins, the sins of my parents and ancestors.

Blood of Jesus, let my body, soul and spirit be cleansed and purified from every pollution that I have inherited, or suffered, in the Name of Jesus.

Holy Spirit, reveal and defeat all selfishness in me, in the Name of Jesus.

Every anti-God and anti-Christ spirit hindering my spiritual walk and spiritual growth in God, be separated from me, and die, in the Name of Jesus.

Inherited idols, acquired idols, transferred idols that have ever received worship from me, or now want worship from me, Blood of Jesus, silence those idols and let them DIE, in the Name of Jesus.

Powers pushing me into idolatry especially where it concerns money and its handler, Mammon, DIE, in the Name of Jesus.

My life, receive Fire, become Fire, in the Name of Jesus.

Evil thoughts and imaginations sponsoring demons in my life, perish, in the Name of Jesus.

Unholy cravings and desires sponsoring demons in my body or soul, perish, in the Name of Jesus.

> The generous soul will be made rich, and he who waters will also be watered himself. (Proverbs 11:25)

Every need in my life that is making me do ungodly things, Blood of Jesus, let that need die, in the Name of Jesus.

Lord, every idol *god* that I ignorantly worship, let that worship die, in the Name of Jesus.

Lord, every idol *god* that I silently worship, let that worship die, in the Name of Jesus.

Every idol *god* that I secretly worship, let that worship die, in the Name of Jesus.

Lord, every idol *god* that I unknowingly, unconsciously worship, let that worship die, in the Name of Jesus.

Idol *gods* of my ancestors, die, in the Name of Jesus.

Idol *gods* of my place of birth, die, in the Name of Jesus.

Idol *gods* of my place of origin, die, in the Name of Jesus.

Idols of my father's house, be dethroned from my life, Lord let those *idols* die, in the Name of Jesus.

Idol *gods* of my place of residence, die, in the Name of Jesus.

Idols of my workplace, die out of my soul, in the Name of Jesus.

Lord, any *idol god* that I inherited from my birth, let that idol die, in the Name of Jesus.

Lord, any *idol god* that I serve because of my father's house, let that idol die, in the Name of Jesus.

Lord, by my sacrifice, I give Mammon a bill of divorce and dethrone it from the seat on my heart, in the Name of Jesus.

I consecrate all my gain to Jehovah and desolate the throne of Mammon that has been in my life, in the Name of Jesus.

Lord, I repent of all idolatry, every *idol god* including Mammon, in the Name of Jesus.

Without those *idols*, Lord, I enter into the Kingdom of God, I enter into right relationship with Christ, in the Name of Jesus.

I enter into the blessings and benefits of being one of Yours, Father, in the Name of Jesus.

Lord, trust me with wealth and true riches, and add no sorrow with it for the blessings of the Lord maketh rich and You add no sorrow with it, in the Name of Jesus.

I worship You Lord, in the beauty of Your holiness.

Goodness, and Mercy will follow me all the days of my life.

Money will come up to me to serve me, in the Name of Jesus.

I am in Christ, let every other union with any other *gods* of my father's house, my mother's house, or Mammon, let those connections and unions DIE, in the Name of Jesus.

I am in Christ, let every *spirit of poverty*, *need*, *lack*, *insufficiency*, *fear*, *loneliness*, even married but feeling single, die, in the Name of Jesus.

Lord, let all initiations and rituals binding me to Mammon **perish**, in the Name of Jesus.

Worship coming out of me that is not to God, die, in the Name of Jesus.

Worship coming out of my life to make me idolatrous, DIE, in Jesus' Name.

Anything in my hand that is anti-destiny and is quenching or grieving the Holy Spirit, die, in the Name of Jesus.

Anything in my house that is anti-destiny and is quenching or grieving the

Holy Spirit, Lord let it be revealed to me so I may remove it, in the Name of Jesus.

Whatever they do to prosper in my father's house, but I cannot, I AM IN CHRIST--, let that thing Die and let my prosperity appear, in the Name of Jesus.

I seal these declarations across every dimension, age, era, and timeline--, past present and future, to infinity, in the Name of Jesus. I seal them with the Blood of Jesus and the Holy Spirit of Promise, in the Name of Jesus.

Any retaliation because of this Word, these prayers and this deliverance, backfire 7 times, in the Name of Jesus.

Dear Reader:

Thank you for acquiring and reading this book. I pray it has been a blessing to you and will change how you see and do things, spiritually, for the better.

May God bless you in your Christian walk, and may you never lack any good thing in life.

In the Name of Jesus,

AMEN.

Dr. Marlene Miles

Other books by this author

(the books on finance are pictured with links)

AK: The Adventures of the Agape Kid

AMONG SOME THIEVES

Ancestral Powers

Barrenness, *Prayers Against*
https://a.co/d/feUltIs

Battlefield of Marriage, *The*

Beauty Curses, *Warfare Prayers Against*

Blindsided: *Has the Old Man Bewitched You?*

https://a.co/d/5O2fLLR

Break Free from Collective Captivity

Churchzilla, The Wanna-Be, Supposed-to-be Bride of Christ

Courts of Marriage: Prayers for Marriage in the Courts of Heaven (prayerbook)

Courtroom Warfare @ Midnight (prayerbook)

Curses of Blind Men

Demonic Cobwebs (prayerbook)

Demonic Time Bombs

Demons Hate Questions

Devil Loves Trauma, *The*

Devil Weapons: Unforgiveness, Bitterness,…

The Devourers: Thieves of Darkness 2

Do Not Swear by the Moon

Don't Refuse Me, Lord (4 book series)

https://a.co/d/idP34LG

Dream Defilement

The Emptiers: *Thieves of Darkness, 1*
https://a.co/d/5I4n5mc

Every Evil Bird

Evil Touch

Failed Assignment

Family Token (*forthcoming*)

Fantasy Spirit Spouse

FAT Demons (The): *Breaking Demonic Curses*

The Fold (5 book series)

    The Fold (Book 1)

    Name Your Seed (Book 2)

    The Poor Attitudes of Money (3)

    Do Not Orphan Your Seed (4)

    For the Sake of the Gospel (5)

My Sowing Journal

Fruit of the Womb: *Prayers Against Barrenness 2*

Gates of Thanksgiving

got HEALING? Verses for Life

got LOVE? Verses for Life

got HOPE? Verses for Life

got money? https://a.co/d/g2av41N

How to Dental Assist

How to Dental Assit2: Be Productive, Not Wasteful

I Take It Back

Irresistible: Jesus' Triumphal Entry

Legacy

Let Me Have A Dollar's Worth (mini book)
https://a.co/d/h8F8XgE

Level the Playing Field

Living for the NOW of God

Lose My Location
https://a.co/d/crD6mV9

Man Safari, *The*

Marriage Ed. Rules of Engagement & Marriage

Made Perfect in Love

Money Hunters: Beware of Those

Money on the Altar https://a.co/d/4EqJ2Nr

Mulberry Tree

Motherboard (The) - *Soul Prosperity Series*

Name Your Seed

Occupy: *Until I Return*

Plantation Souls

Players Gonna Play

Power Money: Nine Times the Tithe

https://a.co/d/gRt41gy

The Power of Wealth *(forthcoming)*

Powers Above

The Robe, Part 1, The Lessons of Joseph

The Robe, Part II, The Lessons of Joseph

Seasons of Grief

Seasons of Waiting

Seasons of War

Second Marriage, Third~~, Any Marriage

Sift You Like Wheat

Spirits of Death, Hell & the Grave, Pass Over Me and My House

Soul Prosperity soul prosperity series 3

https://a.co/d/5p8YvCN

Souls Captivity soul prosperity series 2

The Spirit of Poverty

StarStruck

SUNBLOCK

The Swallowers: *Thieves of Darkness*, 3

Take It Back

This Is NOT That: How to Keep Demons from Coming at You

Throne of Grace: Courtroom Prayer

Time Is of the Essence

Too Many Wives: *Why You Have Lady Problems*

Tormenting Spirits
https://a.co/d/dAogEJf

Toxic Souls

Triangular Power *(series)*

    Powers Above

    SUNBLOCK

Do Not Swear by the Moon

STARSTRUCK

Uncontested Doom

Unguarded Hours, *The*

Unseen Life, *The* (forthcoming)

Upgrade: How to Get Out of Survival Mode

    Toxic Souls (Book 2 of series)

    Legacy (Book 3 of series)

Warfare Prayer Against Beauty Curses

Warfare Prayer Against Poverty
https://a.co/d/bZ611Yu

The Wasters: *Thieves of Darkness*, Bk 2
https://a.co/d/bUvI9Jo

What Have You to Declare? What Do You Have With You from Where You've Been?

Spirits of Death, Hell & the Grave, Pass Over Me and My House

Soul Prosperity soul prosperity series 3

https://a.co/d/5p8YvCN

Souls Captivity soul prosperity series 2

The Spirit of Poverty

StarStruck

SUNBLOCK

The Swallowers: *Thieves of Darkness*, 3

Take It Back

This Is NOT That: How to Keep Demons from Coming at You

Throne of Grace: Courtroom Prayer

Time Is of the Essence

Too Many Wives: *Why You Have Lady Problems*

Tormenting Spirits
https://a.co/d/dAogEJf

Toxic Souls

Triangular Power *(series)*

    Powers Above

    SUNBLOCK

Do Not Swear by the Moon

STARSTRUCK

Uncontested Doom

Unguarded Hours, *The*

Unseen Life, *The* (forthcoming)

Upgrade: How to Get Out of Survival Mode

> Toxic Souls (Book 2 of series)
>
> Legacy (Book 3 of series)

Warfare Prayer Against Beauty Curses

Warfare Prayer Against Poverty
https://a.co/d/bZ611Yu

The Wasters: *Thieves of Darkness,* Bk 2
https://a.co/d/bUvI9Jo

What Have You to Declare? What Do You Have With You from Where You've Been?

When I Was A Child, *I Prayed As a Child*

When the Devourer is Rebuked
https://a.co/d/1HVv8oq

When You See Blood

The Wilderness Romance *(series)* This series is about conducting a Godly relationship and marriage with someone who is a Wilderness person. It is about how to recognize it and navigate through it. These books are about how not to get caught up in such.

- *The Social Wilderness*
- *The Sexual Wilderness*
- *The Spiritual Wilderness*

Credits

Prayers mostly by Pastor Dr. Anthony Akerele

Mountain of Fire Ministries, *The gods and Your Needs*
https://www.youtube.com/watch?v=gmNKpAppqTo

Power Money: 9x the Tithe by Dr. Marlene Miles
https://a.co/d/0vYc2q1

Art: Adapted from Dreamstime.com

www.ingramcontent.com/pod-product-compliance
Lightning Source LLC
LaVergne TN
LVHW021408080426
835508LV00020B/2509